Make it
HAPPEN

Alfredo Quiñones

SURGEON

BY DAN GUNDERMAN

Lightswitch
LEARNING

150 East 52nd Street, Suite 32002
New York, NY 10022
www.lightswitchlearning.com

Educators and Librarians, for a variety of teaching resources, visit www.lightswitchlearning.com

Library of Congress Cataloging-in-Publication Data is available upon request.
Library of Congress Catalog Card Number pending

ISBN: 978-1-68265-581-8

2 3 4 5 6 7 8 9 10

Dr. Alfredo Quiñones by Ryan Hume

Edited by Lauren Dupuis-Perez
Book design by Sara Radka
The text of this book is set in Minion Pro Regular.

Printed in China

Image Credits

Cover: Newscom, NOTIMEX
Page 1: See credits for cover
Page 4: Getty Images, Blend Images RM
Page 4: Getty Images (all)
Page 5: (middle) Getty Images, iStockphoto; (top) Getty Images; (bottom) Newscom, NOTIMEX
Page 6: Getty Images, John Moore
Page 7: Getty Images
Page 8: Getty Images, Moment Open
Page 9: Getty Images, Moment RF
Page 10: Getty Images, iStockphoto
Page 11: Getty Images, Gary Gershoff
Page 12: Getty Images, Justin Sullivan
Page 14: Getty Images, iStockphoto
Page 15: Getty Images, iStockphoto
Page 16: Getty Images
Page 18: Getty Images, iStockphoto

Page 19: Getty Images, iStockphoto, (back) Cultura RF
Page 21: Getty Images, (bottom) Justin Sullivan, (top) Science Photo Library RF
Page 22: Getty Images
Page 23: Getty Images, iStockphoto
Page 24: Getty Images, Creatas RF
Page 25: Getty Images, Tetra images RF
Page 26: Getty Images, iStockphoto
Page 27: Getty Images, Cultura RF
Page 28: Getty Images, Radius Images
Page 29: Getty Images, Tetra images RF
Page 30: Newscom, NOTIMEX
Page 31: Getty Images, Blend Images
Page 32: Getty Images, Science Photo Library RF
Page 33: Getty Images, iStockphoto
Page 34: Getty Images
Page 35: Getty Images

Page 36: Getty Images
Page 37: Getty Images
Page 38: Getty Images, Caiaimage
Page 39: Getty Images
Page 40: Newscom, NOTIMEX
Page 41: Getty Images
Page 42: Getty Images, iStockphoto
Page 44: Getty Images, iStockphoto
Page 45: Getty Images, U.S. Navy
Page 46: Newscom, MCT
Page 47: Getty Images, Hero Images
Page 48: Getty Images, (top) Image Source; (bottom) Newscom, NOTIMEX
Page 49: (middle)Getty Images, (top and bottom) iStockphoto
Page 50: Getty Images, Justin Sullivan
Page 51: (left and right) Newscom, NOTIMEX

"I enjoyed every step
because I knew it was leading
to something bigger."

Dr. Alfredo Quiñones-Hinojosa

• • •

Make It! HAPPEN!

Activities

Both searching for and working toward a career can be challenging work. This recurring feature at the end of each chapter will help readers build toward career readiness. The "Make it Happen" activity will tie relevant information from every chapter into ideas about career readiness. It will enable readers to more easily reach a variety of goals to ensure success in school and in the community.

Contents

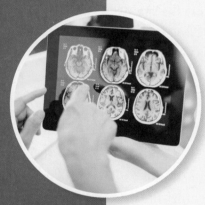

Introduction

At midmorning inside an **operating room** at the Mayo Clinic in Jacksonville, Florida, Dr. Alfredo Quiñones-Hinojosa lifts his bulky eyewear and lowers his surgical mask. He's just finished a successful surgery. He has removed a cancerous **tumor** from a patient's brain. As the patient heads to the recovery room, Dr. Quiñones-Hinojosa is off to check in with the patient's family. After that he will prepare for another surgery.

Dr. Quiñones-Hinojosa, known as Dr. Q, has had a successful career that grew from a humble beginning. He had nothing but $64 and a dream when he came to the United States as a teenager in the late 1980s. With **perseverance** and confidence, he spent almost 20 years pursuing an education. As a grad student, he chose medicine instead of law. Now he is a well-known brain surgeon and researcher. He helps save lives while also researching new ways to fight cancer. His life has been filled with struggles, triumphs, and mentors who helped him reach his goals.

This book will show how a person can achieve goals through support from their community and with a strong sense of self. Dr. Q's journey did not come without great challenges. By overcoming them, he became the caring doctor patients around the world admire today.

Each year many people come to the United States to work on farms and in factories for very low wages.

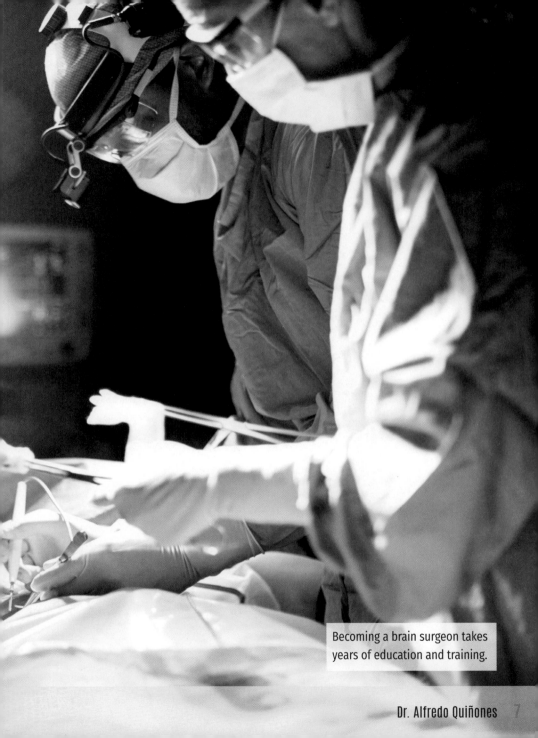

Becoming a brain surgeon takes years of education and training.

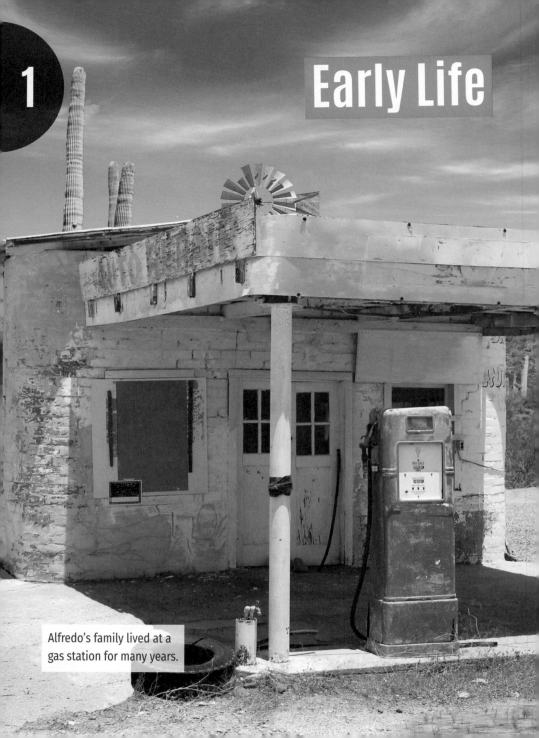

1

Early Life

Alfredo's family lived at a gas station for many years.

Who is Alfredo?

Alfredo was born in Mexico in January 1968. He had a large family, and was the oldest of six children. He lost a younger sister to colitis, a condition that affects the colon.

Alfredo grew up near Mexicali, an area just south of California. His family worked hard. They often struggled when his father's business didn't do well. His dad owned a gas station, and the Quiñones family lived in an apartment in the back of the station. Alfredo started working there when he was only five years old. Because of the poor **economy** in Mexico, Alfredo's father was forced to sell the gas station for almost no profit. Meanwhile, the Quiñones family barely had enough money to eat.

In the 1980s, Mexico experienced a financial crisis. Because of it, life changed for Alfredo's family. The peso, which is the type of money used in Mexico, lost value. This meant it was not worth very much. Buying everyday things became difficult because prices skyrocketed. During this time, Alfredo sold hot dogs on the street corner to help his family.

Previously, when his dad's business had been doing well, Alfredo and his family would enjoy meat once per week. But by the 1980s, Alfredo's family had to survive on flour tortillas and homemade salsa. They had very little money.

Tortillas are made with flour or corn, salt, water, and oil.

Without the correct tools, like gloves, pulling weeds can be very difficult.

Hard Work

When Alfredo was about 14, he began taking short trips to California to work. He helped his Uncle Fausto, who worked on a ranch in the San Joaquin Valley. Alfredo spent two months there working in the sun, pulling weeds. His goal was to earn some money to help support his family.

In a 2012 interview with CNN's Sanjay Gupta, Alfredo said, "I remember [. . .] my hands, the very same hands that now do brain surgery, right around that time, they had scars everywhere from pulling weeds. They were bloody."

Hands are a surgeon's most valued instrument. If Alfredo's hands had been permanently damaged in the fields, he might not have become a successful surgeon.

The experience was eye-opening for Alfredo. It taught him what it was like to work long hours. It also taught him how to develop communication skills, and how to **adapt** to new situations. "That hard-earned cash proved that people like me were not helpless or powerless," he later wrote, according to CNN.

Even though he worked hard in the fields, he still had time to dream. During this time, he wanted to become an elementary school teacher. He enrolled at a teacher-training college in Mexico. He did very well in school. He graduated when he was only 18. Soon after, Alfredo began teaching in a rural area of Mexico. Unfortunately, the pay was too low to live. He had to return to Fausto's ranch for a short period. There, he earned extra money on top of his teacher's salary.

The Dog Expert

Alfredo and other immigrants to our nation worked hard to overcome personal challenges and build new lives. Like Alfredo, Cesar Millan moved from Mexico to California to find work. He lived on the streets of San Diego and found a job grooming dogs. It was soon clear that he had a powerful talent that helped him understand dogs. He moved to Los Angeles to wash cars and work with dogs. On the side, he began a dog rehabilitation service. He also took on extreme cases of dogs that misbehaved. Today, he works to make sure that dogs are trained safely to live with people and other dogs.

Cantaloupe can be exhausting to farm, as the crop is very heavy.

Changing Focus

Alfredo's family continued to struggle. He felt that it would be helpful if he went to college in the U.S. He also knew he had family there. If they let Alfredo work with them, he would be able to earn some money for college.

By 1987, the economy in Mexico had worsened. If Alfredo wanted to fulfill his dream to improve his education, he would have to take the **initiative** to move to the U.S. At the age of 19, he knew it was time to leave Mexicali and move to Fresno, California. There, he worked very long hours under the hot sun to save enough money to continue his education.

At first, when he hardly had any resources or money, Alfredo worked at any job he could find. He was **creative** in finding work. His jobs included picking a variety of crops, such as cantaloupe, cauliflower, and corn. He even had a job cleaning petroleum tanks. While in the U.S., he quickly learned to speak English. He also learned about different parts of American culture. But Alfredo's main goal was to earn money for food.

DID YOU KNOW?

In 2015, 15 percent of all immigrants given lawful residence in the U.S. were Mexican. That means 3 out of every 20 immigrants were from Mexico.

CRASH COURSE IN SURGERY

anesthesiologist: a doctor who manages a patient's pain during and after surgery

internship: a job for a recent graduate in order to gain experience

MCAT: Medical College Admission Test, a national test required for attending medical school

neurobiology: a branch of science focusing on the anatomy of the nervous system

neurosurgeon: a surgeon with a specialty in treating issues affecting the nervous system and the brain

post-doctoral work: mentored research or training to gain more experience in a certain specialty

residency: a period when a doctor receives advanced training at a hospital

scientific journal: a publication that reports new research in science or medicine

tumor: an abnormal growth of tissue

There are more than 77,000 farms in California.

Working to Help Others

In an interview many years later with the television reporter Brian Lamb, host of C-SPAN's program *Q&A*, Alfredo noted, "All I wanted to do was work hard enough so I would have food on the table for myself, my future children, my parents, and my siblings. And that's exactly the journey that I took all the way from back then until where I am today."

> **"All I wanted to do was work hard enough so I would have food on the table for myself, my future children, my parents, and my siblings."**
>
> **ALFREDO QUIÑONES**

Alfredo's heart and spirit were much too strong to quit after those challenging early days after he came to the U.S. Even though the work with Fausto and the stress of his move was difficult, Alfredo always focused on having a plan to become successful. But success meant something special to Alfredo. He wanted to be able to work to help others.

As a young boy with big goals and dreams, Alfredo had seen how difficult it was for a family like his to be able to afford food and a house to live in. He knew how demanding work could be for many different groups of people. What followed was a journey that took him from being a poor boy in Mexico to becoming a medical school graduate and successful doctor.

Make It! HAPPEN!

Make a Travel Itinerary

In his life, Alfredo had to travel from one country to another, and then to different states in the U.S. By traveling to different places close to home or far away, people can learn about new cultures and new opportunities. Select a place you would like to visit, and research the specifics of the trip. Then create a spreadsheet on the different costs involved:

- Transportation (bus or train ticket, rental car)
- Lodging (hotel, bed and breakfast, or staying with friends and family)
- Food (three meals per day)
- Miscellaneous expenses (souvenirs, gifts, etc.)

How much would a three-night trip cost? What about a five-night trip? Discuss how you could adjust the budget to make travel more affordable.

2

First Steps of the Journey

ERECTED BY
JANE K SATHER
MDCCCCVIIII

More than 40,000 students are enrolled at
the University of California, Berkeley. Only
17.5 percent of applicants are accepted.

Working for a Purpose

A t age 19, Alfredo came alone to a new country to build a new life. He didn't have any friends yet and he couldn't speak English. What was he to do? Luckily, he was such a driven and inspired person that there was only one thing he could do. He worked and studied hard to earn money and accomplish his goals.

According to his personal website, he once said, "I had big dreams, and I would rather risk my life than stay in Mexico . . . I never felt like my life was hard, though. It was a privilege for me to be here. I enjoyed every step because I knew it was leading to something bigger."

He worked tirelessly, seven days per week. He told a reporter at *The New York Times* newspaper that after a year of working as a cotton picker, painter, and **welder**, he moved to Stockton, California. There, he got a job loading freight cars and completed other difficult, labor-heavy tasks. All of them required long hours.

Remembering those difficult times, he continued, "My eyes burned from the sulfur, and my clothes smelled from fish [oil], but it paid me enough so that I was able to go to night classes at San Joaquin Delta Community College."

Encouraged by his advisors and teachers, he submitted his application to the University of California-Berkeley. At age 23, Alfredo's dreams and goals to go to a four-year college and get a good job were being realized.

Student Life

Once Alfredo became a student at UC Berkeley, he didn't forget those long, hot days working in the fields. His field jobs had taught him what hard work looked like. This work ethic carried over to his studies and the way he treated others. He told C-SPAN's *Q&A* host Brian Lamb, "You know, I think the American Dream comes back to the [. . .] principle of hard work."

At the university, he studied **psychology**. According to his personal website, Alfredo struggled with speaking and writing assignments because he was still learning how to speak English. So, he adapted and took classes that did not require too much writing, such as calculus, physics, and chemistry, to keep his grade point average up. Still, he continued to work hard to practice his English.

Despite moving from farm worker to advanced student, Alfredo's personality never changed. He was still the kind, caring, and passionate person he had been while growing up at his family's gas station, teaching in rural Mexico, and plucking weeds in the California sun.

Alfredo studied hard and hoped to have a stable profession. When deciding between a career as a lawyer or a doctor, Alfredo considered his own family's past. His grandmother was a *curandera*, or village healer. He was inspired by her story, and soon chose medicine because he too wanted to help other people.

A scalpel is a small and extremely sharp blade used for surgery. It can make very clean and precise cuts in the skin.

Brain Mapping

Different parts of the brain control different parts of the body. The brain even controls parts of our personality and, of course, memory. During some brain surgeries, patients are awake. This allows the doctors to monitor how the operation is impacting different parts of the brain. Below is an explanation of each part and what they control.

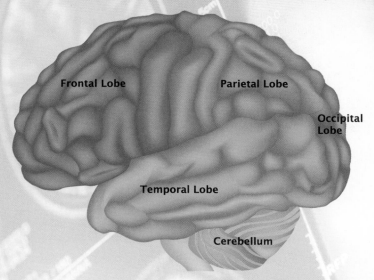

Frontal Lobe

Parietal Lobe

Occipital Lobe

Temporal Lobe

Cerebellum

FRONTAL LOBE
The frontal lobes control problem solving, memory, language and judgment.

PARIETAL LOBE
The parietal lobes interpret sensation and help people interpret what they are experiencing.

OCCIPITAL LOBE
This lobe is the visual processing center for the body.

TEMPORAL LOBE
This lobe processes hearing. It connects meaning to the sounds we hear.

CEREBELLUM
The cerebellum controls voluntary movement, such as balance and coordination.

At Harvard Medical School, there were more than 720 medical students enrolled in 2017.

Discovering the Brain

nce in medical school at Harvard University, Alfredo began to discover his career focus. He was drawn to surgery, and soon that interest would become even more specific. One day, one of his professors invited him to watch a brain surgery. In describing this experience to the *Q&A* host Brian Lamb, Alfredo said, "Some things happen for a reason. And I used to think that chance and good luck come to anybody who wants it. But I began to realize that it's not just that. It comes to those who look for it. And one day, I was walking in the hallways of Harvard Medical School and a very, very **distinguished** brain surgeon looked at me on a Friday night around 11:00 p.m., and he asked me, 'Where are you going?' And I said, 'I'm going to the library to study.' And he said, 'Have you ever seen brain surgery?' And I said, 'No.'"

The doctor then invited Alfredo to watch an actual operation. "Imagine the magic that I felt when I saw that beautiful brain on a patient that was awake; which is incidentally what I do nowadays," Alfredo told Lamb. "One of my specialties is doing brain surgery and taking tumors from patients that are awake."

He described the surgery he witnessed in 1997 as "beautiful." He said the brain had a rhythm that "danced with the heart." Because blood flows through the main organs, the brain seemed to have a

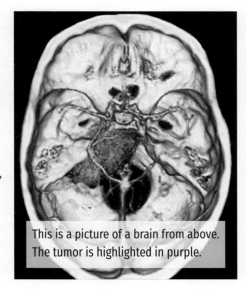

This is a picture of a brain from above. The tumor is highlighted in purple.

pulse, which allowed Alfredo to see the body "at work," or "in motion." He said he completely loved the idea of surgery after that moment.

Love and Marriage

Dr. Q first met his wife, Anna Peterson, while still learning English in community college. At the time, he was a member of the track and field team and was recovering from an injury when Anna said "hi" to him. The two started dating when Alfredo was at UC Berkeley, one year before Harvard University. Anna followed him to Harvard, and they married in 1996. Today, they have three children between 12 and 18 years old.

Brain Surgeon

Several years later, in 1999, Alfredo graduated with honors and gave the **commencement** speech for his medical class at Harvard University. He had become Dr. Quiñones-Hinojosa, or

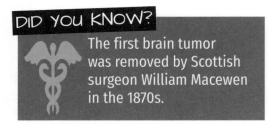

Dr. Q. Over the next six years, Dr. Q completed his **internship**, **residency**, and additional work that helped him become a neurosurgeon. These are steps that doctors must take to reach the top of their field. Each step takes years. Finally, in 2005, Johns Hopkins University Hospital in Maryland hired him as a specialist in brain tumor surgeries.

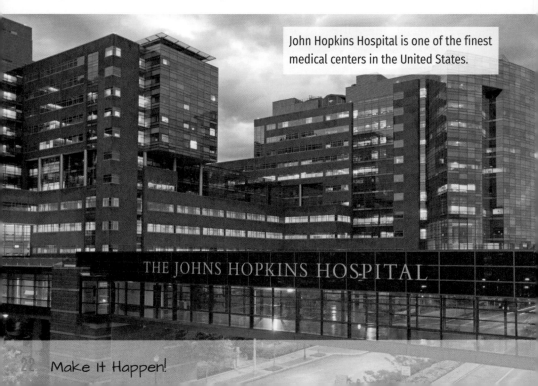

John Hopkins Hospital is one of the finest medical centers in the United States.

THE JOHNS HOPKINS HOSPITAL

Make It! HAPPEN!

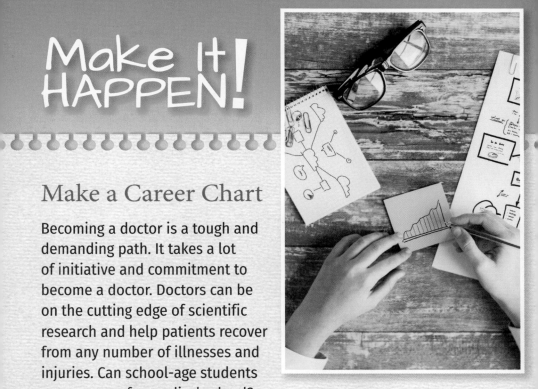

Make a Career Chart

Becoming a doctor is a tough and demanding path. It takes a lot of initiative and commitment to become a doctor. Doctors can be on the cutting edge of scientific research and help patients recover from any number of illnesses and injuries. Can school-age students prepare now for medical school?

You can start by developing an understanding of what doctors do. There are many types of doctors, including:

- Surgeons
- Physicians
- Pediatricians
- Oncologists
- Cardiologists
- Dentists

Create a "compare and contrast" chart of the skills it takes to be each kind of doctor. How do they align with your interests? What do the professions have in common?

3

Overcoming
Obstacles

Medical students spend many hours studying
and working. It is tiring and difficult work.

A Physical Test

D r. Q experienced many different hardships on his long and difficult journey to success. The test of someone's true character is often whether or not they can persevere. Over time, Dr. Q learned to work hard and managed to overcome his challenges, one by one.

In his life, Dr. Q has overcome some physical obstacles to reach where he is today. One in particular shaped his early adult years, taught him about health, and even helped guide his career.

On April 14, 1989, while cleaning out tanks that once held petroleum, Dr. Q fell to the bottom of one of the tanks. At that time, Dr. Q was 22, working and paying his way through school. He was repairing a valve in a tank when he went inside to retrieve an item that had fallen in. His coworker, Pablo, warned him it was too dangerous.

A stethoscope is one of the first tools a medical student needs. It is used to listen to a patient's heart and lungs.

Alfredo learned a life lesson after falling into a tank and almost dying.

Fumes from the petroleum residue nearly knocked him out. "I thought that I could actually be a superhero, like my idol Kalimán, from a Mexican comic book I grew up reading as a kid," he said in 2013. But he was wrong. He was breathing in the poisonous ingredients in gasoline. He became dizzy and his vision was blurry. He became very confused. He almost died. Dr. Q tried with all his might to climb a rope back up and grab Pablo's hand. However, he slipped and tumbled to the bottom of the tank before passing out. "I registered falling slowly, everything encased in darkness," he said in the speech. "My father heard the crash, and my body reverberated in the tank." He has described this as a moment that changed his life. He grew from this "fall" because he held himself accountable for his mistake and was able to learn from it.

How to Become a Doctor

COMPLETE A 4-YEAR COLLEGE DEGREE
(Majoring in the sciences is helpful.)

APPLY TO MEDICAL SCHOOL
(You will need to take a test called the MCAT to get in. The better your score, the better school options you have.)

COMPLETE MEDICAL SCHOOL
(four years)

COMPLETE A RESIDENCY PROGRAM
(Depending on your specialty, this can last 3-8 years.)

OBTAIN A MEDICAL LICENSE
(You need a special license to practice medicine.)

CONGRATULATIONS!
You're a doctor!

Receiving help from a doctor was an important moment in Dr. Q's life.

There Are No Accidents

Dr. Q does not believe in accidents. For him it was a turning point, as well as a learning experience. Soon, he woke up in a hospital. Beside him was a doctor. "I have learned that the answers are [. . .] found during challenging times, when you fail and you have to get up and try again," he told students during a commencement speech.

But the obstacles Dr. Q has faced go further than just physical challenges. There were also many people who didn't believe Dr. Q would ever go to college. Many times the insults were related only to stereotypes, or sets of ideas and assumptions people sometimes have about others.

> **"**I have learned that the answers are [. . .] found during challenging times, when you fail and you have to get up and try again.**"**
>
> **ALFREDO QUIÑONES**

There were even those within his own family who believed he would never do anything but pull weeds. Dr. Q's cousin was a source of doubt and negativity. While Dr. Q was working in the fields, his cousin told him that "this is your future!" However, Dr. Q knew he could prove people wrong by continuing to reach for his goals.

His success was also questioned by strangers. There were people who assumed he would never amount to anything just because he was a young farm worker. They also assumed he could never achieve his dreams because of where he was from. This sort of verbal bullying continued through his school years and even into his career.

Types of Bullying

Bullying can be classified into four different types:

1. **Physical bullying** occurs when someone is hit, kicked, punched, tripped, etc.

2. **Verbal bullying** occurs when someone calls another person a foul name, or insults, teases, intimidates, or calls someone out.

3. **Social bullying** can be done "behind the scenes," or behind someone's back. It is when someone's reputation is hurt or smeared, or people spread questionable rumors about another person. It often results in the victim being humiliated.

4. **Cyber bullying** is conducted online or over the phone. This form of bullying has become prevalent in schools around the world.

Overcoming Self-Doubt

In his 2013 commencement speech to Johns Hopkins University students, Dr. Q told students that he experienced bullying while in college. "Early on, I was afraid of my future, made to feel insecure." He went on to explain, "At times, I was embarrassed of my roots, hesitant to tell people [about my origins]." But it never slowed down his strong work ethic and his rapidly improving **problem-solving** skills in science. The mean comments from people in his life did not change his course. Dr. Q did not give up his dream of helping others.

His path to success didn't look like everyone else's. But his time in medical school wasn't all negative. Dr. Q told CNN's Sanjay Gupta that often, while in medical school, he had to stop and look at everything around him. He still wanted to soak it all in. He couldn't believe how far he had come.

Referring to the doubts and the bullying, Dr. Q told Lamb, "I don't shy away from it. I welcome it. I realize that [. . .] what I thought was a weakness—that I came as a poor immigrant and now I was a brain surgeon—turned out to be the greatest strength of my life."

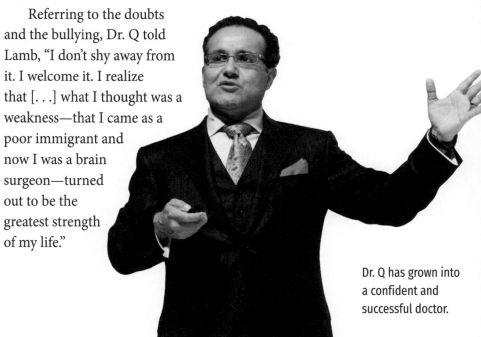

Dr. Q has grown into a confident and successful doctor.

Make It! HAPPEN!

Reflect on Overcoming Challenges

Achieving your goals will not happen without some sacrifice or difficulties that you'll need to overcome. All people have conflicts and barriers to overcome. Obstacles will be different depending on what you're trying to achieve. You could find obstacles to overcome in:

- School, as you try to make it into a good college
- Sports, as you try to make the team, advance to varsity, or win the championship
- School activities, as you try out for the lead role in the school musical
- In preparation for standardized testing, like the PSATs or SATs
- Moving to a new city or town

Write a short essay about three different obstacles you have already faced in your own life. How did you get through them? How did they change you? What skills did you need to succeed?

4 Teamwork

Successful doctors are built with the help of a team of experts that help them along the way.

Dr. Q's Community

Day in and day out, Dr. Q works with and speaks to many different people. He depends on his work team for their medical knowledge. They **collaborate** to help people and save lives. His team helps him continue to develop as a brain surgeon.

The team around Dr. Q isn't just made up of those dressed in medical scrubs who join him in the operating room. It also includes the family members who encouraged him or helped him along his journey. His wife is a huge part of his team. She supported him while he was spending his days and nights working in the hospital. Dr. Q's children are also crucial, for they have become a reason he continues to work hard to find a cure for cancer. He also often recalls all the mentors who helped him get into quality schools and conduct important research.

Teamwork is one of the most important portions of Dr. Q's life. A part of being a teammate is assisting others, but also having others assist you in return.

> **DID YOU KNOW?**
>
> According to the Bureau of Labor Statistics, there is expected to be an 18 percent increase in the need for surgeons in the next decade.

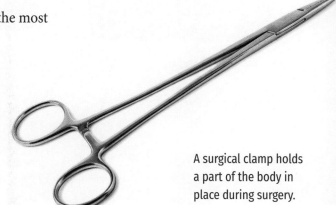

A surgical clamp holds a part of the body in place during surgery.

The Help of Mentors

Many different people played a part in helping Dr. Q throughout his journey. His uncle Fausto helped him when he was young. In fact, Fausto gave the future Dr. Q his first taste of the American dream. It was clear to Dr. Q that he would have to work hard if he was going to fulfill his dream of an education. The days with Fausto taught him that he could accomplish anything he put his mind to. This mentality later helped him in his medical career.

Finding a mentor who wants to help you achieve your goals is a great way to build a community.

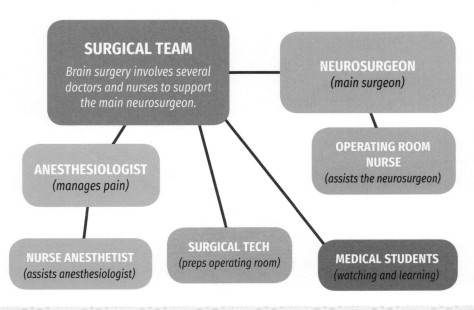

SURGICAL TEAM
Brain surgery involves several doctors and nurses to support the main neurosurgeon.

NEUROSURGEON
(main surgeon)

OPERATING ROOM NURSE
(assists the neurosurgeon)

ANESTHESIOLOGIST
(manages pain)

NURSE ANESTHETIST
(assists anesthesiologist)

SURGICAL TECH
(preps operating room)

MEDICAL STUDENTS
(watching and learning)

There have also been several inspirational figures in Dr. Q's medical life that have pushed him to excel. These people continued to believe in him and encourage him toward excellence.

Norm Nichols, the speech and debate coach at San Joaquin Delta Community College, took Dr. Q under his wing and helped him in college. "He took me into his family and mentored me," Dr. Q told Claudia Dreifus of *The New York Times* newspaper. "Norm helped me apply for and get accepted to the University of California, Berkeley."

Dr. Q's personality was a big part of why he succeeded. People wanted to help him. Dr. Q met Joe Martinez during his undergraduate studies. Martinez became his mentor in the psychology department. He also introduced Dr. Q to the **neurobiology** lab at the school. It was Martinez who encouraged him to apply to Harvard University Medical School.

Plastic Surgery

Plastic surgeons help repair or replace skin and muscles. "Plastic" relates to the Greek word meaning "to mold." It describes the surgeon's role in moving tissue around to achieve a certain appearance. In regards to brain surgery, plastic surgeons can be an important part of the surgery team. They understand how to reduce scarring after surgery. A scar is a mark left on the body after an injury, such as a cut, has healed. This can be important when operating on the head or face. Plastic surgeons can also repair the skull after a surgery on the brain.

Most people do not want to look different, especially if they are undergoing a scary procedure. Fighting tumors or cancer can cause a person a lot of stress. Looking different after surgery can add to that stress. Plastic surgeons can help patients look the same as they did before. By understanding the shape of a person's head, or the best way to place a scar so it is less visible, plastic surgeons can help patients feel and look better.

Medical Community

Doctors all come from a variety of backgrounds and have made a great impact on the medical field and the world around them. They are constantly working together to discover new techniques. The medical community encourages diverse thinking and continuous problem-solving. There is more than one way to be a successful doctor.

DR. REGINA BENJAMIN

UNIVERSITY OF ALABAMA AT BIRMINGHAM

In 2002, Dr. Benjamin became the first African American woman to be the president of the state medical society of Alabama. In 2009, she was appointed by President Barack Obama to be the nation's surgeon general (serving until 2013).

DR. ROD ROHRICH

BAYLOR COLLEGE OF MEDICINE

Dr. Rohrich has been recognized for his work in plastic/reconstructive surgery and education, and he is considered one of the best surgeons in the U.S. In addition to performing surgeries, Dr. Rohrich is a professor at the University of Texas Southwestern Medical Center at Dallas.

DR. MEHMET ÖZ

UNIVERSITY OF PENNSYLVANIA SCHOOL OF MEDICINE

Dr. Öz is one of the most recognizable medical professionals. The Turkish-American is a cardiothoracic surgeon and professor at Columbia University, and hosts a popular daytime talk show, "The Dr. Oz Show."

DR. SANJAY GUPTA

UNIVERSITY OF MICHIGAN MEDICAL SCHOOL

Dr. Gupta is a neurosurgeon and CNN's chief medical correspondent. He is also the associate chief of neurosurgery at Grady Memorial Hospital in Atlanta, Georgia, and an assistant professor at Emory University School of Medicine.

DR. MOHAMED ZAYED

WASHINGTON UNIVERSITY IN ST. LOUIS

Dr. Zayed was one of the 2017 recipients of the American Surgical Association Foundation Fellowship. He splits his time between operating on patients and researching blood flow and veins. He is currently researching how to reduce the chances that someone with diabetes will lose a limb.

Working As a Team

Dr. Q also works closely with his surgical team. In the challenging position of a brain surgeon, he depends on **teamwork** for much of his success. He must work and communicate with a large medical staff to bring about the best results for his patients. Complicated medical procedures cannot be done alone. They are often serious, high-risk surgeries that require careful attention and monitoring.

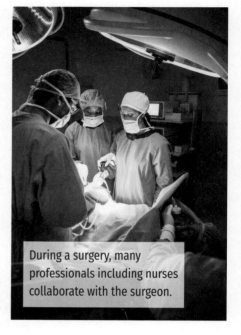

During a surgery, many professionals including nurses collaborate with the surgeon.

During the 2011 C-SPAN *Q&A* interview, Dr. Q told Lamb, "Yesterday morning I did a case that lasted about 12 hours and [. . .] I was the captain of this team and I had two ENT [ear, nose, and throat] surgeons, or otolaryngologists [specializing in the head and neck], I had two plastic surgeons, and then I was leading a team of neurosurgeons, obviously."

Dr. Q is quick to recognize the other professionals on his medical teams. Another part of what determines true greatness is the ability to take feedback, be collaborative, and continue to look ahead at what the future holds. Much of what Dr. Q does requires help and knowledge from fellow doctors. His diverse team is made up of people who have also studied in college or medical school. It includes other neurosurgeons, plastic surgeons, anesthesiologists, nurses, and hospital staff who all work together.

Make It! HAPPEN!

Build a Personal Network

Networking is an important skill to have when meeting people who have similar interests.
People network at school, at work, and when enjoying sports or other activities. When meeting people in your network:

- Maintain eye contact with the person you're speaking with
- Consider the other person's point of view
- Ask questions that can benefit everyone involved
- Use many different networking methods, including in-person networking and virtual networking on social media, websites, and forums

Who do you know in your community that you can network with? Networking can be important when applying to colleges. Talk to friends and family about networking opportunities. Maybe someone you know can introduce you to an important future contact to help you learn more about a college or help you find a job.

Current Career

Dr. Q continues to push boundaries with his work. He is always looking for ways to fight brain cancer and brain-tumor growth.

New Challenges

Dr. Q's career has continued at a fast pace. From medical procedures to parenting three children, he is a busy man. The most recent news in his life includes switching hospitals. In 2016, he took a new job at the Mayo Clinic in Jacksonville, Florida. He had been at Johns Hopkins University for over a decade.

In his new role, he is continuing his clinical care, research, and teaching at Mayo. "The Mayo Clinic is an outstanding institution that is now opening its doors for our family to come and be a part of a dream to make this world a better place," Dr. Q wrote in a letter posted on the Latino Medical Student Association website in 2016.

He added, "I will continue to be equally or more active as a physician and surgeon and as a teacher and student. I will now have the opportunity to learn from a new group of colleagues."

Experiencing new perspectives is important as a doctor. Interacting with and learning from new people can help spark new research. It can also lead to new collaboration opportunities.

Jacksonville, Florida

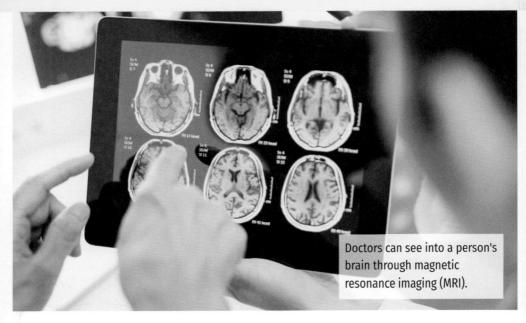

Doctors can see into a person's brain through magnetic resonance imaging (MRI).

Fighting Cancer

Every day, Dr. Q works to advance what we know about cancer. He has made this his life's work. He often experiences moments that remind him how harmful the disease is. To show this, he uses the case of Chris, a patient of his several years ago. He spoke about this in a speech to Johns Hopkins University students in 2013.

He first met Chris in 2011. Dr. Q said that the man's tumor was "massive and dangerous." It stretched through a large portion of his brain. Dr. Q called the area "no man's land." It was an area that was very difficult to operate on.

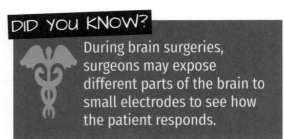

DID YOU KNOW?

During brain surgeries, surgeons may expose different parts of the brain to small electrodes to see how the patient responds.

"When you go to remove a tumor in that part of the brain, it's like defusing a ticking time bomb," Dr. Q said in his 2013 speech. He compared the surgery to a scene from the film *The Hurt Locker*, when a character disarms a bomb. That is the sort of adrenaline rush that comes during tough brain surgeries.

"Just like that [. . .] the world in which Chris and I lived collapsed," Dr. Q said in his speech. Something went wrong. A cluster of blood vessels burst. Chris suddenly lost more than four liters of blood. "[Chris's] life was literally escaping in front of me. Was I afraid? Yes, I was afraid. If you're not afraid that you might fail, you may not get the job done."

Annual Salaries by Specialty

SPECIALTY	ANNUAL SALARY
Orthopedics	$443,000
Cardiology	$410,000
Neurosurgeon	$384,000
Plastic Surgery	$355,000
General Surgery	$322,000
Family Medicine	$207,000
Pediatrics	$204,000

During this moment, Dr. Q remembered the words of Cesar Chavez, the well-known twentieth-century Mexican American farm worker. Chavez was also a civil rights leader who worked hard to protect the rights of other farm workers in the country. "If you are afraid, you will work like crazy," Chavez said.

Chris ended up surviving—tumor-free—and was able to be with his wife again. Dr. Q called it a "magical moment."

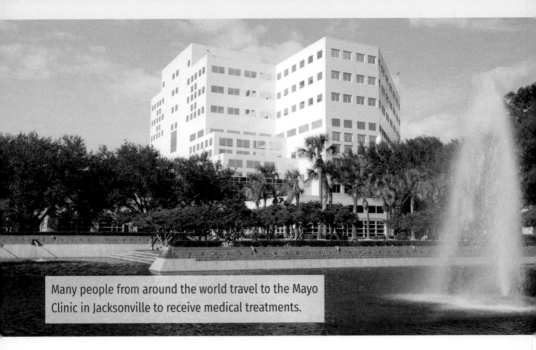

Many people from around the world travel to the Mayo Clinic in Jacksonville to receive medical treatments.

Balancing Family

Dr. Q's life at home is also very important. While he admitted to being "spent" at times when his children wanted to play when they were young, he tried—and still tries—to be around for them whenever he can. So while he continues to pioneer treatment at the Mayo Clinic, he still makes room for family.

Dr. Q's days are long and could be filled with consultations, discussions with families, or research work. At one point in his early career, Dr. Q was spending 120 to 140 hours per week on the job. He told C-SPANS's Brian Lamb that his children thought he lived at the hospital.

DID YOU KNOW?

Stem cells, which can be found throughout the body, can generate replacements for bone and muscle cells.

Here is how Dr. Q once described his day: First he'd begin by running at around 5:00 a.m. Then he would make office calls and go to the operating room. He would not get home until around 8:00 p.m. He'd enjoy dinner with his children for 30 minutes, tell them a story, put them to bed, and go back to his office until 10:30 p.m. When he returned home, he'd spend an hour with his wife watching the news. Adding to his workday, he would also have to be on call for his patients throughout the night.

About this hectic schedule, Dr. Q told Lamb, "I'm human, of course I get tired [. . .]. Every morning when I get up at 5 a.m. my body aches, you know, and I'm sore because I've been training and I am tired but [. . .] I think about all those patients that are struggling every day, and as soon as I do that, I get up and it's like the world starts."

Mission: BRAIN Foundation

Dr. Q is also the co-founder and president of Mission: BRAIN (Bridging Resources and Advancing International Neurosurgery), a foundation created in 2011. Mission: BRAIN was organized to help people who have limited access to doctors, medicine, and health care in general. It aims to bring neurological education and expertise to people around the world. For example, in Haiti, Mission: BRAIN will help bring much-needed medical attention and resources where only two neurosurgeons serve the entire population of over 10 million.

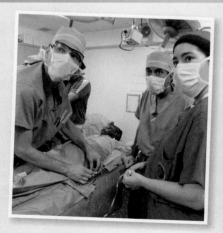

Stem Cells

Dr. Q's research work is another important part of his life. It may even impact future generations. He is working on a new way to fight cancer. The method uses stem cells to identify and combat the cancer cells. Stem cells can grow into any kind of cell in the body. They can be transplanted into patients who have been treated for cancer in order to grow healthy cells. This technique is still being studied closely.

On his website, Dr. Q states that he "believes that there are natural stem cells in the brain that, if put in just the right spot, could halt the spread of cancerous cells in the brain, working more effectively and naturally than any surgery or [treatment] currently in use." Dr. Q has said that he hopes cancer becomes an illness that is as inconvenient as the common cold.

Most recently, he is also helping to develop a different kind of procedure for brain-tumor removal. As explained in a video posted to YouTube, Dr. Q said that surgeons can collaborate with plastic surgeons to operate through the eyelid, through a "narrow corridor," to get at the cancerous mass. He indicated that it takes a lot of teamwork because the plastic surgeon needs to be precise with each incision, and the brain surgeon has little space to work in. However, Dr. Q said that it can help reduce scarring and get patients back to their lives quicker!

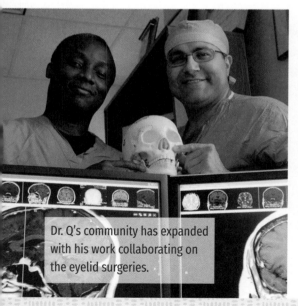

Dr. Q's community has expanded with his work collaborating on the eyelid surgeries.

Make It! HAPPEN!

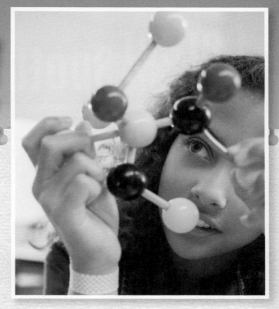

Build a Research Plan

Successful people often conduct research to help them make smart decisions about reaching their goals. People do research on a wide variety of topics, including jobs, term papers, medical conditions, and when preparing to compete against others in sports or debates. To be a good researcher:

- Check sources to make sure they are accurate
- Ask good questions to get good results and information for your research
- Be persistent to search for the correct information to better understand your subject
- Be patient, as good researching takes time and persistence
- Understand ownership and make sure to give credit to sources and the ideas of others
- Network online and in person to help gather and share information

What topics would you research to learn more about different careers? How would you share your research with others?

Career Spotlights

Dr. Q is a humble person who studied for almost 20 years and worked hard to become a kind and caring surgeon. Here are some specific highlights from his successful career to date:

Graduate

In 1994, Dr. Q graduated with highest honors from UC Berkeley. He graduated cum laude from Harvard Medical School in 1999.

Winner

In 2006, he was named the winner of the Franklin Martin Faculty Research Award by the American College of Surgeons.

Becoming Dr. Q

In 2011, he published his memoir, *Becoming Dr. Q*.

Professor

In 2012, Dr. Q was promoted to full Professor at Johns Hopkins University.

Mayo Clinic

In 2016, Dr. Q joined the staff at Mayo Clinic to continue his work in saving people's lives.

Defining Moments

At the age of nineteen, Alfredo makes a tough decision to leave his home country and move to California, where he finds work to help his family.

1987

Alfredo falls into a deep petroleum tank while making a repair. Although he fell unconscious and had to be rescued by his coworker and his dad, he woke up in the hospital, surrounded by doctors, whom he admired. He believes this was a life-changing event that made him a bit more humble.

1989

Alfredo attended medical school, where he learned about diversity, criticism, advanced science, and networking with other professionals.

Late 1990s

2005

Alfredo, or Dr. Q, begins his tenure at Johns Hopkins University and begins to research a cure for brain cancer.

2011

Dr. Q starts the organization Mission: BRAIN to help patients around the world, especially those in "underserved" areas.

Today

Dr. Q continues to consider his family members to be his heroes. He still strives to be the best dad and husband he can be.

Depth of Knowledge

1   Explain how Dr. Q's opening quote to this book—"I have learned that the answers are [. . .] found during challenging times, when you fail and you have to get up and try again"—is illustrated in the text.

2   The author emphasizes the importance of perseverance, optimism, and collaboration. What other central themes can you identify? How and where are the themes expressed?

3   Write a list of Dr. Q's important life and career skills that have contributed to his success. Use specific examples from the book.

4   Use the information you have learned in this book to craft a story of an imagined patient for Dr. Q, from the initial consultation to the surgery to the recovery room.

5   Choose one of Dr. Q's peers from the Medical Community section (pgs. 36–37). Conduct a research project to answer the following questions: What challenges have they overcome? How does their work help people today? Formulate three additional questions about your chosen medical professional and write an essay answering them.

Host a Networking Event

To help you meet your goals, you can host an event specifically geared toward meeting other people with similar goals. With a group of your peers, plan and host a networking event.

MATERIALS NEEDED

- Cardstock and pens, or a computer and printer
- An indoor or outdoor event space
- Refreshments

STEPS TO TAKE

1 Form a small group with classmates that share similar interests. Collaborate to choose a topic for your networking event.

2 Assign jobs for event planning. Each member should be responsible for an important aspect of the event.

3 Create invitation cards, by hand or on the computer. Invite guests, including people you do not know. Ask guests to RSVP, as this will help you with event details.

4 Prepare your venue. Whether it is indoors or outdoors, it should be comfortable and look nice. Provide drinks and snacks.

5 Mingle. Take initiative and meet everyone. Refer to Chapter 4's Make It Happen for suggestions.

6 Afterward, meet with your planning team and discuss your event. What worked? What didn't? What could you improve on for next time?

Glossary

adapt *(verb)* to change your behavior so that it is easier to live in a particular place or situation (pg. 11)

anesthesiologist *(noun)* a doctor who manages a patient's pain during and after surgery (pg. 13)

collaborate *(verb)* to work with another person or group in order to achieve or do something (pg. 33)

commencement *(noun)* a ceremony for students who have graduated from a school or college (pg. 22)

creative *(adjective)* having or showing an ability to make new things or think of new ideas (pg. 13)

distinguished *(adjective)* known by many people because of some quality or achievement (pg. 20)

economy *(noun)* the process or system by which goods and services are produced, sold, and bought in a country or region (pg. 9)

internship *(noun)* a job for a recent graduate in order to gain experience (pg. 22)

MCAT *(noun)* Medical College Admission Test, a national test someone applying to medical school needs to pass (pg. 13)

neurobiology *(noun)* a branch of science focusing on the anatomy of the nervous system (pg. 35)

neurosurgeon *(noun)* a surgeon with a specialty in treating issues affecting the nervous system and the brain (pg. 13)

operating room *(noun)* a room in a hospital where surgeries are done (pg. 6)

perseverance *(noun)* the quality that allows someone to continue trying to do something even though it is difficult (pg. 6)

problem-solving *(noun)* the process or act of finding a solution to a problem (pg. 30)

psychology *(noun)* the science or study of the mind and behavior (pg. 18)

residency *(noun)* a period when a doctor receives advanced training at a hospital (pg. 22)

scientific journal *(noun)* a publication that reports new research in science or medicine (pg. 13)

teamwork *(noun)* the work done by people who work together as a team to achieve something (pg. 38)

tumor *(noun)* an abnormal growth of tissue (pg. 6)

welder *(noun)* a person whose job is to join pieces of metal together (pg. 17)

Read More

Christen, Carol. *What Color Is Your Parachute? For Teens: Discover Yourself, Design Your Future, and Plan for Your Dream Job.* Berkeley: Ten Speed Press, 2015.

Etingoff, Kim. *Women Who Built Our Scientific Foundations.* Broomall, Pa.: Mason Crest, 2014.

Hallberg, Bruce A. *Networking: A Beginner's Guide.* New York: McGraw-Hill Education, 2014.

Hauser, Brooke. *The New Kids: Big Dreams and Brave Journeys at a High School for Immigrant Teens.* New York: Free Press, 2011.

Sanders, Stephan. *So You Want to Be a Doctor? The Ultimate Guide to Getting into Medical School.* New York: Oxford University Press, 2014.

Velásquez, Liliana. *Dreams and Nightmares: I Fled Alone to the United States When I Was Fourteen.* West Lafayette, Ind.: Parlor Press, 2017.

Internet Links

http://doctorqmd.com/dr-q-s-story---a-doctor-without-borders/

https://www.c-span.org/video/?301396-1/qa-alfredo-Quiñoneshinojosa

https://www.youtube.com/watch?v=MvRJLpsSBJM

https://www.youtube.com/watch?v=eQF8or9shiQ

www.mayoclinic.org/departments-centers/neurosurgery/home/orc-20117096

http://teacher.scholastic.com/activities/immigration/young_immigrants/

Bibliography

Doctorqmd. "Dr Alfredo Quinones-Hinojosa—CNN interview." *YouTube.* YouTube, 18 May 2012. Web. 22 June 2017.

Dreifus, Claudia. "A Surgeon's Path From Migrant Fields to Operating Room." *The New York Times.* The New York Times, 12 May 2008. Web. 22 June 2017.

Johns Hopkins. "Dr. Alfredo Quiñones-Hinojosa—Johns Hopkins University 2013 Commencement." *YouTube.* YouTube, 25 May 2013. Web. 22 June 2017.

"Dr. Q." *Dr. Q—Dr Q's Story—A Doctor Without Borders.* Dr. Q and the Dr. Q Team, 2017. Web. 22 June 2017.

"Dr. Quinones Moves to the Mayo Clinic." *Latino Medical Student Association at Harvard Medical School.* Latino Medical Student Association, 12 Oct. 2016. Web. 22 June 2017.

"May 2016 National Occupational Employment and Wage Estimates." *U.S. Bureau of Labor Statistics.* U.S. Bureau of Labor Statistics, 31 March 2017. Web. 11 July 2017.

"Q&A Alfredo Quinones-Hinojosa." *C-SPAN.org.* National Cable Satellite Corporation, 7 Sept. 2011. Web. 22 June 2017.

Index